Horse Riding

C O N T E N T S

Introducing ... the Horse 2
Horse or Pony? 4
Dress Sense 6
Fine and Dandy 8
Saddling Up 10
Bridles 12
Bits and Pieces 13
Ready to Ride? 14
On the Move 16
Horses for Courses 18
Can you Hack it? 20
A Day at the Show 22
Caring for a Pony 24
Pony Picking 26
Horsing Around 28
Pick of the Ponies 30
For the Record 31

Collins*Children's Books*

Copyright © HarperCollins Publishers Ltd 1996

Introducing ... the Horse

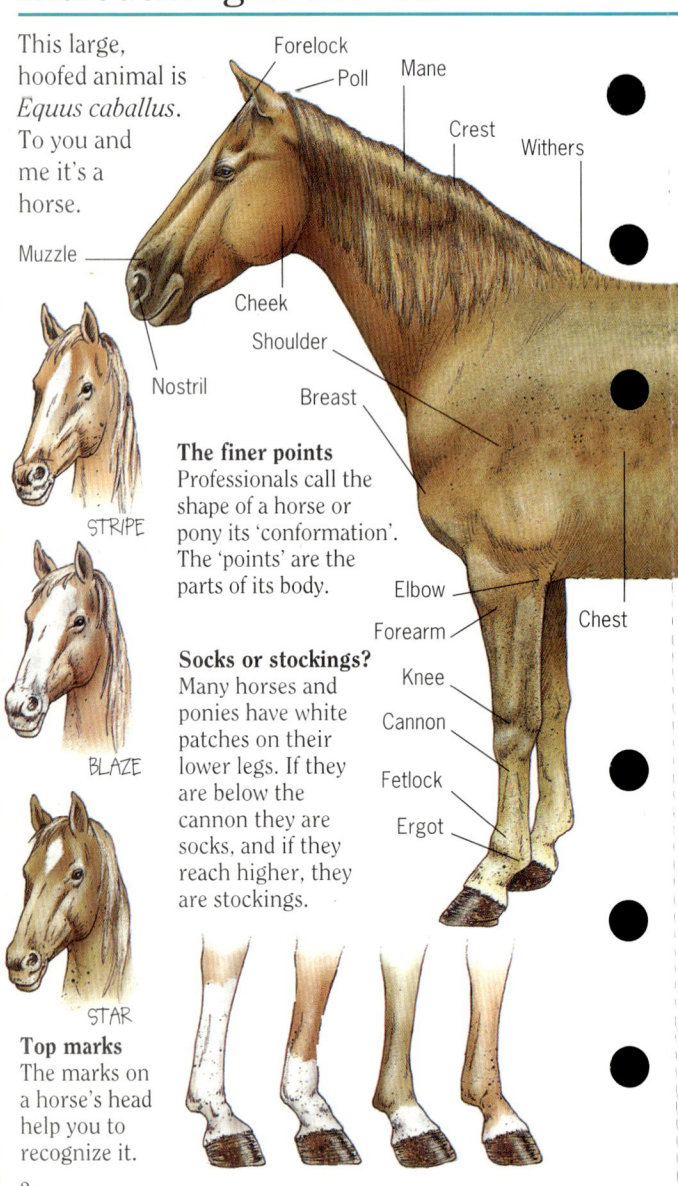

This large, hoofed animal is *Equus caballus*. To you and me it's a horse.

Labels: Forelock, Poll, Mane, Crest, Withers, Muzzle, Cheek, Nostril, Shoulder, Breast, Elbow, Forearm, Chest, Knee, Cannon, Fetlock, Ergot

The finer points
Professionals call the shape of a horse or pony its 'conformation'. The 'points' are the parts of its body.

Socks or stockings?
Many horses and ponies have white patches on their lower legs. If they are below the cannon they are socks, and if they reach higher, they are stockings.

STRIPE

BLAZE

STAR

Top marks
The marks on a horse's head help you to recognize it.

2

Introducing ... the Horse

Curious cousins
You probably know that the ass and the zebra are related to the horse, but did you know that the rhino is too?

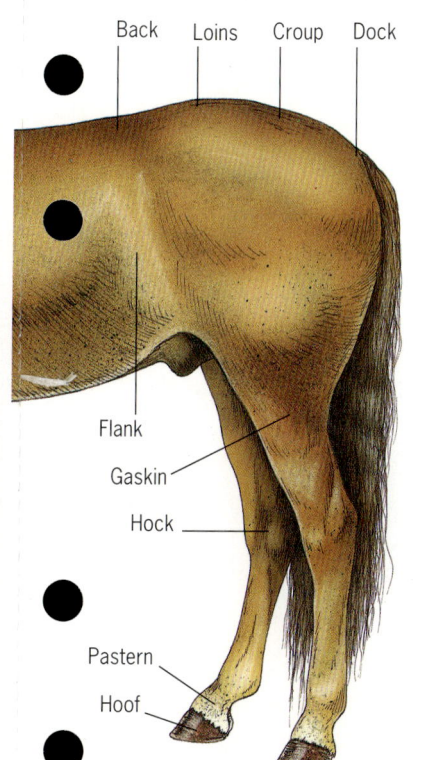

Back   Loins   Croup   Dock

Flank
Gaskin
Hock

Pastern
Hoof

BAY

GREY

STRAWBERRY ROAN

Colour coded
Different colours have different names, but not always the names you'd expect. For instance, a white horse or pony is called a grey.

PALOMINO

3

Horse or Pony?

What distinguishes a horse from a pony? The answer is its height, which is measured in 'hands'. If the animal is shorter than 14 hands and 2 inches it's a pony, and if it's taller it's a horse. Now you know!

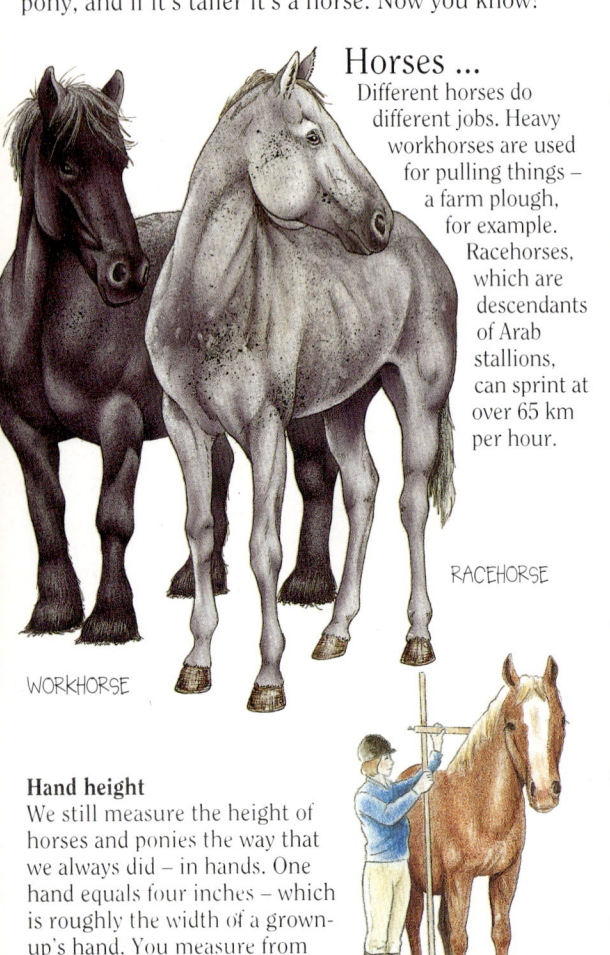

Horses ...

Different horses do different jobs. Heavy workhorses are used for pulling things – a farm plough, for example. Racehorses, which are descendants of Arab stallions, can sprint at over 65 km per hour.

RACEHORSE

WORKHORSE

Hand height
We still measure the height of horses and ponies the way that we always did – in hands. One hand equals four inches – which is roughly the width of a grown-up's hand. You measure from the ground up to the withers (see page 2).

Horse or Pony?

Pick one your own size
Eight- to eleven-year-olds should choose a pony between 11 and 13 hands high. By fourteen you will probably be riding a horse. The important thing is that the animal is the right size for you, and you for it.

... and ponies
Hardy, sure-footed and strong, ponies are perfect for riding on pretty well any terrain.

Hello horse
When you greet your horse or pony make sure it can see you. Don't shout or wave, because a startled animal may kick out or gallop off.

PONY

BITING THE HAND...
Chunks of apple and carrot make great treats for your pony, but watch how you offer them. If your fingers get in the way they'll become an extra pony snack!

Hold your hand out flat with your fingers straight and the food in your palm.

Dress Sense

Let common sense, not fashion fads, dictate what you wear. You must always wear a proper hard hat whenever you ride. Nothing else will protect your head.

Hard hat with chin strap

Hair pulled back off face

The right stuff
Traditional riding clothes are expensive, but they are made to last. You can buy most of the gear second-hand, but don't skimp on the hard hat – buy it new and make sure it's a perfect fit.

Hacking jacket – warm and close-fitting

Jodhpurs – reinforced inside the knee

Knee-high leather or rubber boots with a small heel

RIDE ASIDE!
Up to the 1920s, most ladies rode side-saddle, with both legs on one side of the horse.

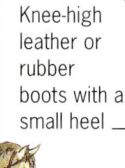

Dress Sense

Everyday wear
You can wear jeans or a tracksuit and a T-shirt so long as they are comfortable and not too baggy or tight. Keep warm in cold weather with a jumper and waterproof jacket. Then all you need is a hard hat and sensible footwear.

FEET FIRST
Riding boots have small heels to stop your feet sliding through the stirrups, but you could wear heeled walking shoes instead. Do *not* wear wellies (they are too loose) or trainers (no heel).

Mudguards
When the Wild West became muddy, men put on thigh-high leggings called 'spatterdash'. Women protected their dresses by stuffing them into wide 'stirrup stockings'.

HAT WITH A HISTORY
Ancient Roman charioteers wore helmets made of bronze with a peak to shield their eyes from the sun. Hard hats have changed little in shape since then!

Fine and Dandy

A groomed pony is a happy pony. Mud and dust make it look a mess. *You* need a wash and brush-up after exercise, and so does your pony.

Good grooming
Grooming is the time to check a pony for any scratches or injuries. If you spot something, ask the vet to check it out.

1 Feet first. Pick out the hoof, working from heel to toe. Get rid of all the grit and dirt that's compacted inside the hoof.

TOOL KIT
HOOF PICK
For picking dirt out of hooves!

DANDY BRUSH
Shifts mud and dirt.

BODY BRUSH
Brings out the shine.

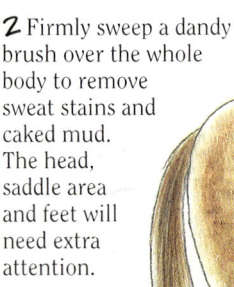

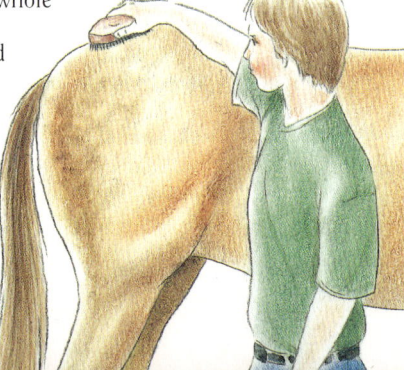

CURRY COMB
Mainly used to clean other brushes.

2 Firmly sweep a dandy brush over the whole body to remove sweat stains and caked mud. The head, saddle area and feet will need extra attention.

3 Next, work from head to tail with the body brush. Its bristles remove dirt and hair from deep in the coat. Scrape the body brush on a curry comb every few strokes to clean it.

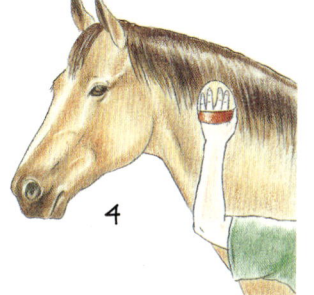

4 For a neat mane, dip a brush in water and brush the the mane flat against the pony's neck.

5 Tail time. A dandy brush will see off those nightmare knots in the tail. Brush it gently, a few hairs at a time – pulling knotty hair hurts ponies too.

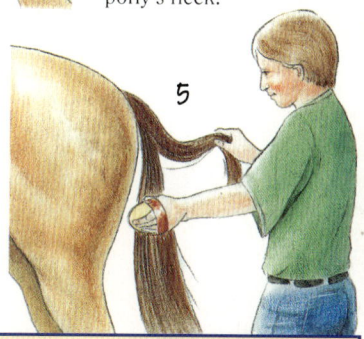

LUCKY HORSESHOES

Did you know the word 'farrier' comes from the Latin, *ferrus*, meaning iron? Farriers are the people who give hooves the monthly beauty treatment. They trim your pony's hooves and replace the shoes, which are made of iron. Each shoe is fixed with seven nails – it's this 'lucky seven' that makes the horseshoe lucky.

Saddling Up

Well you *could* leap up and ride bareback, but with 'tack' riding is a lot easier. Tack is short for tackle, basically it's the saddle and bridle – the items that help you ride a pony.

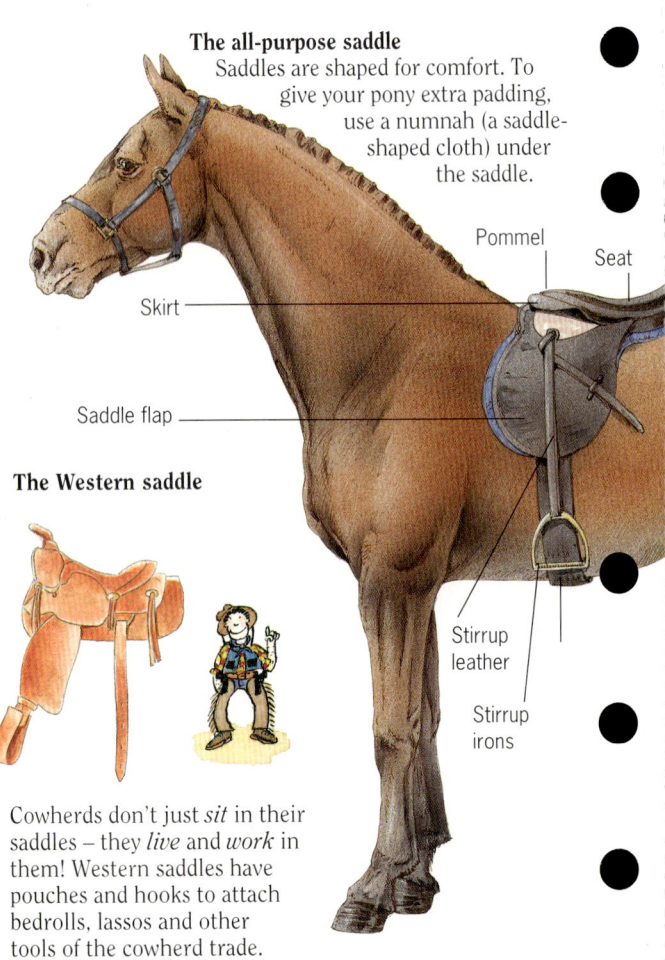

The all-purpose saddle
Saddles are shaped for comfort. To give your pony extra padding, use a numnah (a saddle-shaped cloth) under the saddle.

Pommel

Seat

Skirt

Saddle flap

The Western saddle

Stirrup leather

Stirrup irons

Cowherds don't just *sit* in their saddles – they *live* and *work* in them! Western saddles have pouches and hooks to attach bedrolls, lassos and other tools of the cowherd trade.

Saddling Up

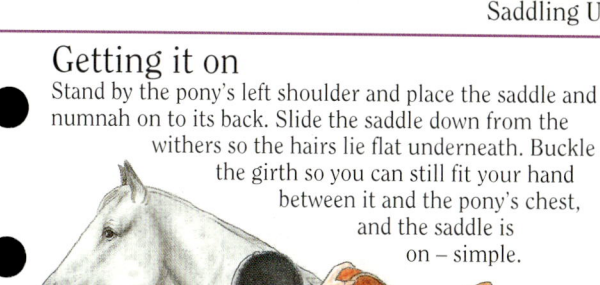

Getting it on
Stand by the pony's left shoulder and place the saddle and numnah on to its back. Slide the saddle down from the withers so the hairs lie flat underneath. Buckle the girth so you can still fit your hand between it and the pony's chest, and the saddle is on – simple.

Cantle

IN THE SADDLE

Your stirrups are the right length if your ankle meets the bottom of the irons when your feet are out of the stirrups.

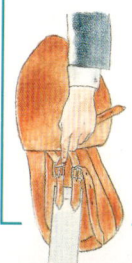

Tighten the girth by one or two holes once you are in the saddle.

Bridles

When you come to put the bridle on, be firm but polite – ponies are not always in the mood to go out. Once it's on, you'll have more control over your pony.

Ask nicely!

Getting it on

1 Reins first. Slip them over the pony's head.

2 Now the bit. Guide it gently into the pony's mouth with your left hand. Take the bridle up over the ears.

3 Is the bit comfortable? Then buckle up the noseband.

4 Finally, fasten the throatlash and check again for fit.

THE BRIDLE
- Headpiece
- Browband
- Cheekpiece
- Noseband
- Bit
- Throatlash
- Reins

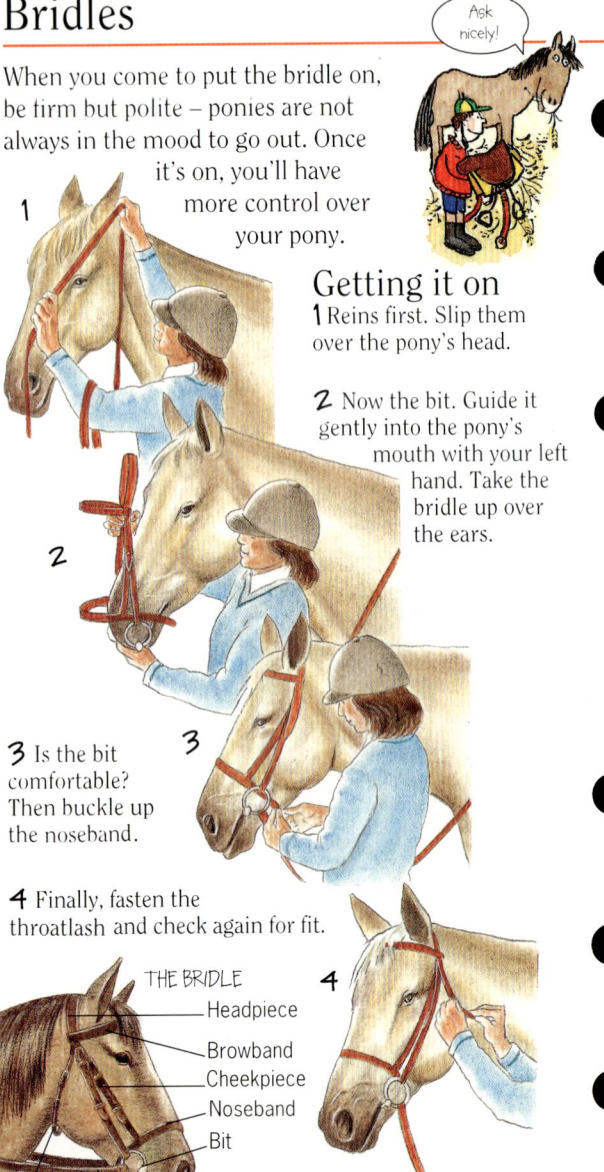

Bits and Pieces

Headgear
You'll use different headgear in different situations – there is no 'all-purpose' headgear.

HEAD COLLAR

Handy to grab on to when catching a pony in a field.

STANDARD BRIDLE

DROP NOSEBAND

Suits most ponies for hacking and jumping.

Allows more control, so it's good for headstrong ponies.

Girths
The girth is the only thing holding your saddle on.

BALDING LEATHER GIRTH

NYLON GIRTH

THREE-FOLD LEATHER GIRTH

Bits
Snaffles are the gentlest bits. There are other bits, used for difficult ponies or in different situations.

Stirrups
Learner riders should use a safety stirrup. Rubber treads prevent your feet slipping.

HALF-MOON SNAFFLE

STANDARD STIRRUP

EGG-BUT SNAFFLE

SAFETY STIRRUP

LOOSE RING SNAFFLE

RUBBER-TREAD STIRRUP

Ready to Ride?

So you're ready to go? How are you going to get on your pony? It's not hard, but there is a technique. Otherwise your charge might charge off without you!

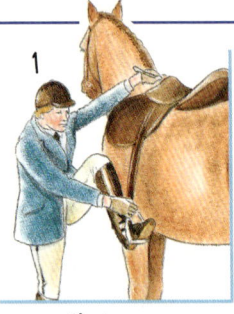

Get on up – mounting
1 Stand by the pony's left shoulder and put your left foot in the stirrup.

2 Kick off with your right foot and pull yourself up by grabbing the saddle.

3 When your left leg is straight swing your right leg over and into the stirrup.

Get on down – dismounting
Take both feet out of the stirrups, swing your right leg behind you and slide down the pony's left side.

Ready to Ride?

Sitting pretty

Keep your head up, back straight, heels down, and your elbows, legs and knees in. Can you remember all that?

Western style
Your back will still be straight, but more relaxed, and your heels and toes will be level.

Reining down
Either reins in both hands, under the middle fingers and over your thumbs and little fingers...

... *or* Western style, held firm in your right hand with your left hand free to throw the lasso!

EQUINE EXERCISES

No, these are not exercises for your pony! They'll keep you fit and supple for painless riding.

Reach with a straight arm to opposite stirrup.

Twist your body around with arms outstretched.

Feet in stirrups, stretch back until you lie down.

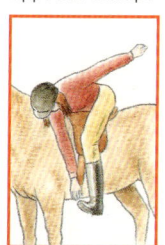

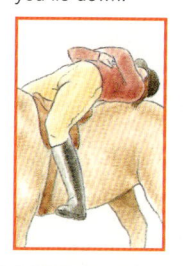

15

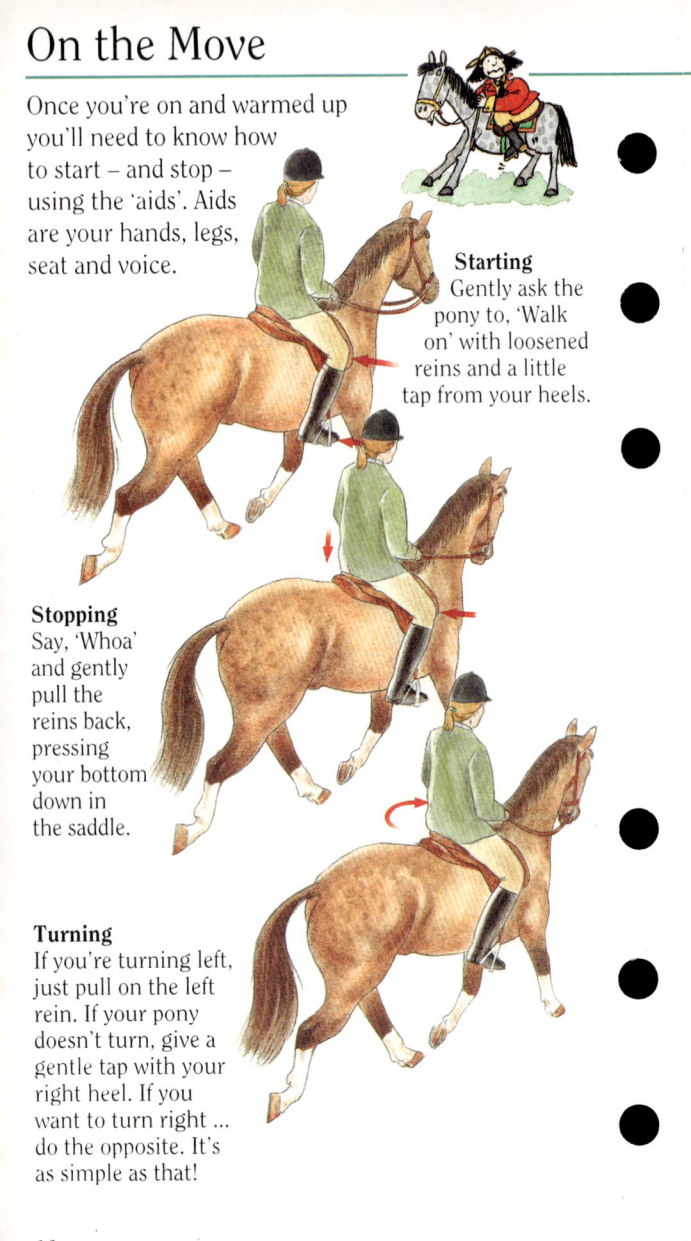

On the Move

Once you're on and warmed up you'll need to know how to start – and stop – using the 'aids'. Aids are your hands, legs, seat and voice.

Starting
Gently ask the pony to, 'Walk on' with loosened reins and a little tap from your heels.

Stopping
Say, 'Whoa' and gently pull the reins back, pressing your bottom down in the saddle.

Turning
If you're turning left, just pull on the left rein. If your pony doesn't turn, give a gentle tap with your right heel. If you want to turn right ... do the opposite. It's as simple as that!

On the Move

The paces
'Paces' are a pony's speeds, from walk to gallop.

Walk has four beats, as the pony places each hoof down separately.

Trot has two beats, as the pony places opposite hooves down together. Back left with front right, then back right with front left.

Canter has three beats, as the pony places a front hoof, then the opposite back hoof, then the other two hooves together.

Gallop has four beats, as the pony places each hoof separately with stretched strides. You will be completely off the ground at one point.

THE MANEGE
This area is used to school ponies and teach riders. This young pony is on a lunge rope, learning to obey the basic voice commands.

Horses for Courses

When it comes to jumping, teamwork is the name of the game. Be confident but cautious, and practise regularly. Always start with the easiest hurdles.

The low down
Trot your pony over very low poles while you both practise keeping your balance and working together.

1

Getting higher
When you're ready, go for it! Increase the distance between the poles until you canter and jump over them.

2

3   4

Fence facts
There are four main types of showjumping fences. If you go to a show, they might not be exactly like these, but look closely and you'll see they are pretty similar.

STAIRCASE

UPRIGHT   TRUE PARALLEL   PYRAMID

18

Horses for Courses

> ## SAFETY FIRST
> - Never go jumping alone. If you fall and hurt yourself you'll need some help.
> - As always, wear a hard hat.
> - Don't forget, your pony might get tired before you do. Ten minutes is enough to start with.

Going through the phases
You might think that a jump is one movement, so let's put you right – there are distinct 'phases' to a jump. Here they are.

1 Approach and 2 Take-off
Work hard at staying balanced – don't lean on the mane or you'll unbalance your pony!

3 Suspension
You are tipped forward in the saddle in mid-air. Remember to stay balanced.

4 Landing and getting away
Swing back into riding position but don't thump down in the saddle – your pony is working hard to move gracefully.

Can you Hack it?

Hacking means cross-country and road riding. There's nothing better than cantering across open spaces on your pony. Follow the Country Code so you and others can enjoy it in the future.

Sights and sounds
Ponies are easily distracted! *You* plan the route, then be firm!

Mmm, yummy smell. Let's go over there!

GOING IN CIRCLES
Taking a wide circular route isn't as silly as it sounds – you can start and finish at the stables. Try to follow the bridle paths where you can, and give the busiest roads a miss.

Hacking heaven
You can have great adventures on a hack, but before you go there are things you must do. Make sure an adult knows where you are going and when you will be back, and stick to your plan. Always take money and a first aid kit.

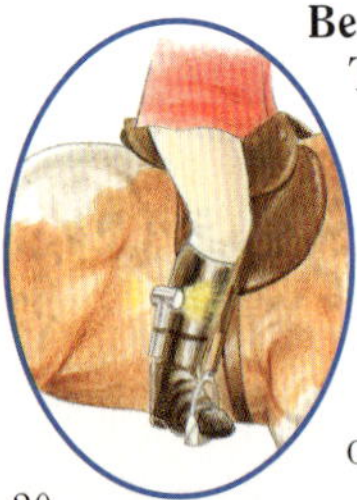

Be sensible and safe
Try to avoid hacking when visibility is poor – in bad weather or at dusk. If you *do* go, use reflectors and stirrup lights to help other traffic see you.

Can you Hack it?

- **On the road**
  If you're on the road, don't forget you're part of the traffic. Stay calm and use the hand signals.

- **On the farm**
  Don't charge through crops! Stick to paths and ride *around* fields. Respect farm animals with their young and watch out for that snorting bull!

The gate code

The rider in front reaches the gate and unbolts it ...

... then opens the gate for the other riders, using the reins to guide the pony back.

The gate is held open until all the riders are through, then it must be closed behind them.

A Day at the Show

1 Yawn ... an early start – I collect Libby from the field.

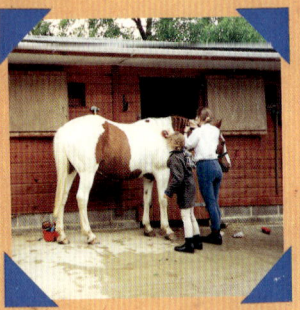

2 Hannah grooms Libby and I plait her mane. She will be perfectly turned out.

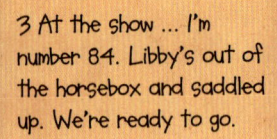

3 At the show ... I'm number 84. Libby's out of the horsebox and saddled up. We're ready to go.

4 Dressage, and Libby performs beautifully.

A Day at the Show

5 On to the jumps, and Libby is jumping brilliantly – don't we look great?

6 The jumping is over. I'm out of breath but really pleased – I think we've done well.

7 Off to the cross-country ... then it's a nerve-racking wait for the judges' decision ...

WE WON!

Caring for a Pony

Okay, you love your pony ... but you can't keep it in your bedroom. If your pony could choose, it would pick a field with other ponies. But what are your choices?

Field ...
An acre of pasture, some shelter, strong fences and a water supply and you have pony heaven – freedom to roam and eat at will.

... or stable
Given plenty of exercise and food, your pony will be happy to live in a stable. Check the hay-net and water are topped up each day.

Mucking out
The grottiest job of them all! If your pony is in a stable, it has to be done each day.

Clear out the dirty straw. Sweep the stable and let it air, then fork the day's fresh straw over the floor.

Caring for a Pony

Nosebag nosh
Give a stabled pony these concentrated foods two or three times a day. In a field, ponies munch all the grass they need.

NUTS   BRAN   HAY   LINSEED   OATS

Hot stuff
A New Zealand rug, with its waterproof outer layer and cosy woollen lining, will keep a pony warm and happy through a chilly winter spell.

Thirsty work
Your pony can drink up to 35 litres of water every day.

Safe and sound
Keep the fences hole-free and padlock the gates.

HACKING HOLS
Pony Clubs hold weekend camps, where you and your pony camp out at night, then hack and hold competitions during the day. The Pony Club will give you information about these. Riding schools may run pony weeks in the holidays. You go to the riding school every day and meet other kids who share your pony passion.

Pony Picking

Picking a pony is not an easy task! They'll all seem lovely! Ask an expert to look at its conformation and a vet to check its health.

A prize pony ...
You want a balanced animal with strong, straight legs. Beautiful big brown eyes and a friendly face are just a bonus.

... and ponies to avoid!
Very few ponies are perfect, but you don't want nags like these ...

Bench knees
The cannon bones turn outwards.

Knock knees
The legs bend in at the knee.

Narrow base
The feet are too close together.

Wide base
The feet are too far apart.

Splayed feet
The feet are turned outwards.

Pigeon toes
The feet are turned inwards.

Pony Picking

A perfect pony
A well conformed pony has prominent withers, a slightly dipped back and a sloping croup.

Backtrack
Stay away from ponies like these – their backs will give you grief.

STRAIGHT BACK

HOLLOW BACK

STRAIGHT CROUP, HIGH-SET TAIL

LOOKING A GIFT PONY IN THE MOUTH

How old is a pony? Ask it to 'Open wide'. Ponies lose their baby teeth by five years, then their big teeth gradually wear down. So check out the teeth to work out the age of your pony.

BIRTH | 6 WEEKS | 9 MONTHS | 6 YEARS | 7 YEARS | 8 YEARS

Horsing Around

Playful ponies like nothing better than to nuzzle and canter with each other. You can learn a lot watching them when they don't know you're there. How busy is your pony's social life?

Muzzle nuzzles
Horses and ponies are sociable animals and benefit from sharing their field with each other. In the wild they would live together in a herd.

Foaling around
Frolicking foals are a delight to watch. They may seem carefree, but a foal's instincts tell it to stay close to its mother for protection.

Horsing Around

Facing facts
Did you know you can tell from a pony's face how it's feeling and what it's thinking? Here's a guide to reading ponies' minds.

ALERT

RELAXED

FEARFUL

AGGRESSIVE

OAPs (Old Age Ponies)
Ponies can live well into their twenties. If they are sharing a paddock, older ponies will have a calming effect on excitable younger ponies, and are perfect for very young children to ride.

Roll up roll up!
There's nothing better than a good roll and back-scratch on a hot summer day – that'll get rid of the flies!

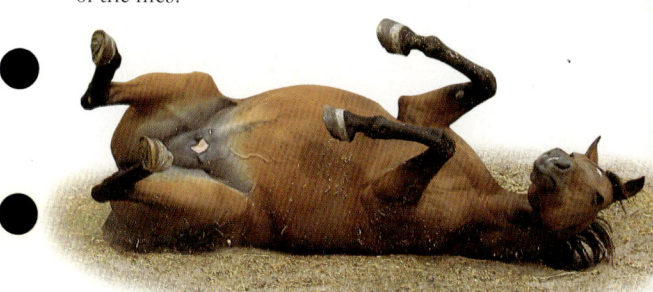

29

Pick of the Ponies

Ponies come from many parts of the world. They share a basic body shape, but each breed has its own special characteristics.

APPALOOSA
A spotty breed from the United States.

SHETLAND
This pony is so small it's measured in inches, not hands. Shetlands are around 40 inches high.

HAFLINGER
Can be either palomino or chestnut, from Austria.

NEW FOREST
Strong shoulders and of mixed descent.

CONNEMARA
From Ireland, these ponies are ace jumpers.

For the Record

PREHISTORIC PONIES
Eohippus (its name means 'dawn horse') was the tiny ancestor of the horse. It lived 58 million years ago, at the time sabre-toothed tigers roamed the land. It had fourteen little hooves, like toenails – four on each front foot and three on each back foot!

Speaking Greek
A chap named Xenophon wrote a book called The Art of Horsemanship around 2,400 years ago – he lived in Ancient Greece. He encouraged riders to understand their horse's temperament and feelings, and to treat them with kindness and respect.

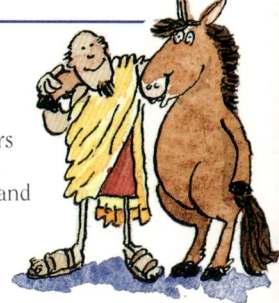

Old nag
The oldest horse we know about was a workhorse called Old Billy, who lived for *62* years, from 1760 to 1822!

Sampson and Pumpkin
A British Shire horse called Sampson was the biggest and heaviest horse on record. Born in 1846 he was 21 hands and 2½ inches high and weighed over 1,500 kg. The smallest was Little Pumpkin, from the United States at just 14 inches high and 9 kg in weight!

Racket the Rocket
A racehorse called Big Racket went like a rocket in Mexico City in 1945. He sprinted at over 69 km per hour!

INDEX

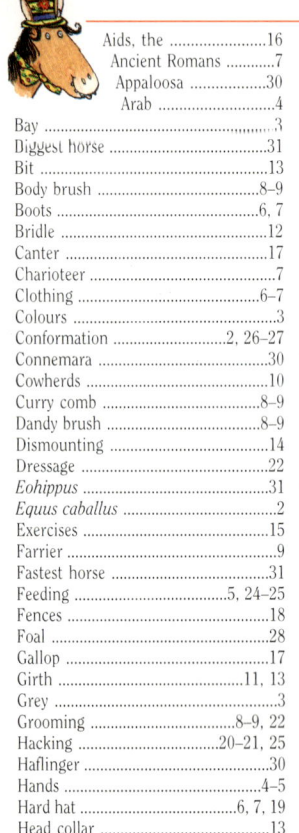

Aids, the	16
Ancient Romans	7
Appaloosa	30
Arab	4
Bay	3
Biggest horse	31
Bit	13
Body brush	8–9
Boots	6, 7
Bridle	12
Canter	17
Charioteer	7
Clothing	6–7
Colours	3
Conformation	2, 26–27
Connemara	30
Cowherds	10
Curry comb	8–9
Dandy brush	8–9
Dismounting	14
Dressage	22
Eohippus	31
Equus caballus	2
Exercises	15
Farrier	9
Fastest horse	31
Feeding	5, 24–25
Fences	18
Foal	28
Gallop	17
Girth	11, 13
Grey	3
Grooming	8–9, 22
Hacking	20–21, 25
Haflinger	30
Hands	4–5
Hard hat	6, 7, 19
Head collar	13
Hoof pick	8
Horseshoe	9
Jumping	18–19, 23
Manege	17
Mounting	14
Mucking out	24
New Forest	30
Numnah	10
Oldest horse	31
Paces	17
Palomino	3
Phases	19
Points	2
Racehorse	4
Records	31
Reins	12, 15
Relatives	3
Riding	14–21
Rugs	25
Saddle	10–11
Shetland	30
Shows	22–23
Sidesaddle	6
Smallest pony	31
Socks	2
Spatterdash	7
Stable	24–25
Stirrup stockings	7
Stirrups	11, 13, 20
Stockings	2
Strawberry Roan	3
Tack	10–13
Teeth	27
Trot	17
Vet	8, 26
Walk	17
Western saddle	10, 15
Workhorse	4–5

Written by Kate Petty
Designed by Ted Kinsey

First published in 1996 by HarperCollins Children's Books,
A Division of HarperCollins Publishers Ltd, 77-85 Fulham Palace Road,
London W6 8JB
ISBN: 0 00 197935 3

Illustrations: Luigi Galante, Aziz Khan and Charlotte Hard

Photographs: Jean-Paul Ferrero/Ardea London Ltd 28c; Helen Elder 22-23; Bob Longrish cover, 8, 20, 24b, 24cl, 28b, 29; Steve Marwood 23; David Miller cover; Mike Roberts/Only Horses 16, 24cr

All rights reserved. No part of this publication may be reproduced, stored in a retrieval system, or transmitted, in any form or by any means, electronic, mechanical, photocopying or otherwise, without the permission of HarperCollins Publishers Ltd

A CIP record for this book is available from the British Library

Printed and bound in Hong Kong